EXPLORE OUTER SPACE

GALAXIES

by Ruth Owen

WINDMILL
BOOKS

New York

Published in 2013 by Windmill Books, An Imprint of Rosen Publishing
29 East 21st Street, New York, NY 10010

Produced for Windmill by Ruby Tuesday Books Ltd
Editor for Ruby Tuesday Books Ltd: Mark J. Sachner
US Editor: Sara Antill
Designer: Emma Randall
Consultant: Kevin Yates, Space Communications Manager, National Space Centre, Leicester, United Kingdom

Photo Credits:
Cover, 1, 4, 6, © NASA; 5 © Flickr (Steve Jurvetson); 7 © ESA/PACS & SPIRE Consortium/ HOBYS Key Programme Consortia; 8 (left), 9 (top), 22–23, 27 © NASA/ESA; 8 (right) © J. Blakeslee (Washington State University); 9 (bottom) © European Southern Observatory (ESO); 10–11, 18–19 © Shutterstock; 12, 17 (right), 24–25 © Science Photo Library; 13 © NASA/JPL–Caltech/R. Hurt (SSC/Caltech); 14 (top) © NASA/ESA/AURA/Caltech, Palomar Observatory; 14 (bottom), 29 © NASA/The Hubble Heritage Team, STScl, AURA; 15 © NASA/ESA/M. Robberto (Space Telescope Science Institute/ESA)/The Hubble Space Telescope Orion Treasury; 16–17, 26 (bottom) © NASA; 20, 21 (Adam Evans) © Wikipedia; 22 (bottom) © NASA/JPL–Caltech/UCLA.

Library of Congress Cataloging-in-Publication Data

Owen, Ruth, 1967–
 Galaxies / by Ruth Owen.
     p. cm. — (Explore outer space)
 Includes index.
 ISBN 978-1-4488-8074-4 (library binding) — ISBN 978-1-4488-8116-1 (pbk.) —
ISBN 978-1-4488-8121-5 (6-pack)
1. Galaxies—Juvenile literature. I. Title.
 QB857.3.O94 2013
 523.1'12—dc23

                                    2011051696

CONTENTS

GOING GALACTIC

If Earth had a space address, it would be "Earth, The **Solar System**, The **Milky Way**, The **Universe**." So what is the Milky Way?

The Milky Way is a **galaxy**. It is a huge collection of **stars**, gas, and dust. Our whole solar system is just a tiny, tiny part of it. If that's hard to imagine, let's do the math.

In 1977, two National Aeronautics and Space Administration (NASA) spacecraft, *Voyager 1* and *Voyager 2*, left Earth. By 2011, *Voyager 1* and *Voyager 2* had made it to the outer regions of our solar system. Even though they were traveling at speeds of about 34,000 miles an hour (54,700 km/h), the two spacecraft still took over 30 years just to reach the edge of our solar system.

Now think about this. The distance across the Milky Way is the same as 50,000 solar systems laid end to end. When it comes to all things **galactic**, huge is seriously huge!

Voyager 2

That's Out of This World!

The original mission of the *Voyager* spacecraft was to visit planets in our solar system and send information back to Earth. Now, the spacecraft are heading out into the Milky Way. Scientists will continue to receive data until contact is lost.

This photo shows the Milky Way from Earth, which is located inside the galaxy.

The Milky Way galaxy is so vast it's hard to imagine anything beyond it. The Milky Way is not alone in space, though. **Astronomers** estimate that there are over 100 billion galaxies in the universe!

Galaxies come in many different sizes. Astronomers believe that some giant galaxies may be home to one hundred trillion stars! Dwarf, or small, galaxies may have only around 10 million stars.

Galaxies are places where stars are born, live, and die—over millions and millions of years. Inside galaxies, stars are born in huge clouds of dust and gas known as **nebulae**. As a nebula begins to shrink under its own **gravity**, it breaks into clumps. These clumps become so hot and dense that they ignite and become stars.

Everything in a galaxy—nebulae, stars, **planets**, dust, and gas—is held together by gravity.

The galaxy named **NGC 4414**

That's Out of This World!

When a star, like our Sun, has burned up all its fuel, it dies. Some stars cool down, fade, and die over millions of years. Others run out of fuel and end their lives suddenly in a huge explosion called a **supernova**.

This bright area is a star forming. It will grow to have 10 times the mass of our Sun.

GALAXIES GETTING IN SHAPE

Galaxies don't just come in different sizes. They can also be described by their shapes.

Spiral galaxies have a circular or disk shape. Arms made of stars branch out from the center of the galaxy. The arms form a shape similar to streams of water spiraling out from a rotating lawn sprinkler.

Barred spiral galaxies have a huge cloud of stars at their center shaped like a football. This star cloud is known as the bar. The galaxy's arms branch out from the ends of the bar.

Elliptical galaxies are vast collections of stars grouped in a round or oval shape. These galaxies look like massive starry soccer balls or footballs.

Bar

Arm

A barred spiral galaxy named **NGC 1300**

An elliptical galaxy named **ESO 325 G004**

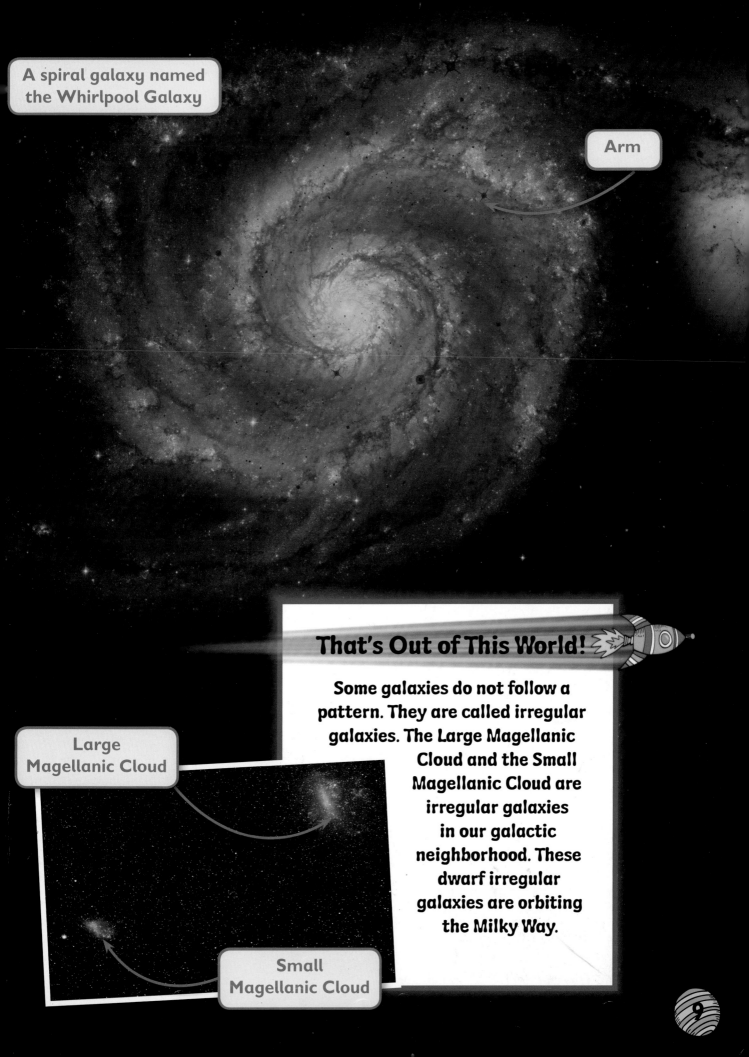

A spiral galaxy named the Whirlpool Galaxy

Arm

Large Magellanic Cloud

Small Magellanic Cloud

That's Out of This World!

Some galaxies do not follow a pattern. They are called irregular galaxies. The Large Magellanic Cloud and the Small Magellanic Cloud are irregular galaxies in our galactic neighborhood. These dwarf irregular galaxies are orbiting the Milky Way.

How to Measure a Galaxy

When we travel on Earth, we measure the distance in miles or kilometers. We can do the same in measuring distances in our solar system. The Sun, for example, is about 93 million miles (149.7 million km) from Earth. When it comes to measuring beyond our solar system, however, the distances are too big to use miles or kilometers.

To measure the size of galaxies and other distances in space, scientists use a unit of measurement called a **light year**. The fastest thing we know of is light. It travels at about 186,500 miles per second (300,000 km/s). A light year is the distance that light can travel in one year.

So if something measured one light year, how long would it be? The answer to that question is about 5,880,000,000,000 miles (9,460,000,000,000 km), or more than 5.8 trillion miles (9.4 trillion km)!

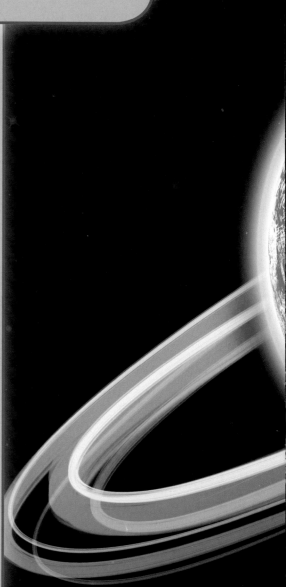

That's Out of This World!

After the Sun, the closest star to Earth is Proxima Centauri. It is 4.24 light years away—the distance that light could travel in 4.24 years. If that doesn't sound so very far, just remember this: Light moves fast enough to travel around Earth seven times in one second!

Our Milky Way galaxy is home to between 200 and 400 billion stars. To cross it, you would have to travel a distance of about 100,000 light years!

The Milky Way is a barred spiral galaxy. The central part of the galaxy is made up of a giant ball of millions of stars called the galactic bulge. Around the bulge, more stars, gas, and dust create a huge disk. The disk has a depth of around 1,000 light years! The galaxy's arms branch out from the disk.

At the center of the bulge is a **black hole**. Astronomers say that this black hole was formed by a massive star that died out and collapsed on itself. This created an incredibly compact, dense object. Its gravitational force is so powerful that nothing in its inner orbit, not even other stars or light itself, can escape being drawn into it!

Galactic bulge

Disk

This artwork shows the Milky Way as if viewed from the side.

This artwork shows the Milky Way as if seen from above.

Arms of stars

Center of galaxy

The bar

The Sun is positioned here within the Milky Way.

That's Out of This World!

Our solar system is orbiting the center of the Milky Way. It takes between 225 and 250 million years for the solar system to make one orbit of our galaxy! Earth is situated about 25,000 light years from the center of our galaxy.

THE STARS OF THE MILKY WAY

The Milky Way contains many star clusters. A cluster is a group of stars that formed around the same time. Each star cluster is held together by gravity.

Open clusters are star clusters with no regular shape. They may contain thousands of stars, or as few as 12.

The Pleiades, or Seven Sisters, is an open star cluster 425 light years from Earth. The cluster contains hundreds of stars, including a small number that can be seen at night without a telescope. The seven brightest stars give the cluster its alternative name of the Seven Sisters.

Globular clusters are balls of stars that are usually around 60 to 100 light years in diameter. A globular cluster may contain as many as one million stars.

M80 is a globular cluster about 28,000 light years from Earth. This cluster is home to hundreds of thousands of stars.

These are the Seven Sisters stars. The two stars shown at the top are seen as a single star when viewed from Earth without a telescope.

M80 globular cluster

That's Out of This World!

About 1,500 light years from Earth, stars are forming in the Orion Nebula. Often called a "star factory," this nebula contains about 1,000 young stars, including four known as the Trapezium. The massive Trapezium stars are 100,000 times brighter than the Sun!

Orion Nebula

The Trapezium stars are in this region of the Orion Nebula.

Stars

Dark Matter

All of the stars, planets, dust, and gas in the Milky Way make up only a small part of the total matter in our galaxy. So what makes up the other part? Right now, scientists don't know the answer to this question!

So how do they actually know something else is out there?

Scientists understand how gravity works. They can figure out how much gravity an object creates and how it affects other objects. Astronomers now know that the gravity created by visible matter is not strong enough to explain how fast our galaxy's stars are moving.

This means there is some other kind of matter out there creating gravity. Scientists have named it **dark matter**.

As yet, scientists do not know what dark matter is. A huge amount of our galaxy and universe is made of something completely new to us!

That's Out of This World!

With 400 billion stars in the Milky Way, astronomers estimate that there must also be billions of planets orbiting those stars. In March 2009, the Kepler space observatory was launched. Its mission is to search for Earthlike planets in the Milky Way that might be able to support life!

Kepler space observatory

The Messier 69 globular cluster of stars is a breathtaking collection of "bright matter." It's the dark matter between and around the stars that is the new challenge for scientists to identify!

LOOKING TO THE STARS

Early astronomers and scientists were aware of the Milky Way long before telescopes were invented. In modern times, however, it has become harder to see the Milky Way with the naked eye. Lights from buildings and cars fill the night sky with a glow that blocks out the wonders of our home galaxy.

It is still possible, however, to view the Milky Way with just your eyes if the conditions are right. You will need to be in the countryside or in an isolated area, such as a desert. Viewing the Milky Way with the naked eye is best done in the summer or winter, on a night with no moonlight.

Seen from Earth with the naked eye, the Milky Way looks like a misty cloud dotted with stars.

That's Out of This World!

From some places on Earth it's possible to see up to 2,000 stars in the Milky Way without using a telescope!

Here is the Milky Way photographed from Arches National Park, in Utah.

MEET THE NEIGHBORS

The Milky Way belongs to a group of around 50 galaxies known as the "Local Group of Galaxies," or "Local Group." The Local Group is about 10 million light years wide!

Just as Earth orbits the Sun, and the Sun orbits the center of the Milky Way, our galaxy and its neighbors are orbiting a central point in the Local Group, all held together by gravity.

The Local Group has two large spiral galaxies, the Milky Way and our nearest large neighbor, Andromeda. Other neighbors include a small spiral galaxy, the Triangulum Galaxy, and the Large Magellanic Cloud and the Small Magellanic Cloud. There are also a number of dwarf galaxies.

The Triangulum Galaxy is nicknamed the Pinwheel Galaxy.

Messier 32 is a dwarf elliptical galaxy.

The Andromeda Galaxy

Messier 110 is a dwarf round or sphere-shaped galaxy.

That's Out of This World!

In galactic terms, "local" can be a long, long way! The Milky Way is around 169,000 light years from the Large Magellanic Cloud. It is about 2.6 million light years from Andromeda.

ANDROMEDA

The nearest galaxy similar in shape to our own Milky Way is the Andromeda Galaxy. Andromeda is also known as Messier 31. Information gathered by NASA's Spitzer Space Telescope suggests that this galaxy may contain around one trillion stars.

Andromeda is larger than the Milky Way with more stars. Scientists believe that the Milky Way has more mass, however, because of the amount of dark matter it contains.

The Andromeda Galaxy is on a collision course with the Milky Way. It is moving toward our galaxy at a speed of around 310,000 miles an hour (500,000 km/h). The two galaxies may eventually collide—in about five billion years! Astronomers believe that if this happens, the two galaxies will merge and form a giant elliptical galaxy.

Andromeda Galaxy

This is an artist's view of the Andromeda Galaxy as seen from its center. A disk of young, blue stars circles the center, with older, redder stars circling farther away.

That's Out of This World!

It is not unusual for galaxies to collide and merge. Over the billions of years that the Milky Way and Andromeda have been in existence, both galaxies have absorbed other galaxies to become the size and shape they are today.

GALACTIC GIANTS

Some groups of galaxies, such as the Local Group, which contains the Milky Way and Andromeda galaxies, are called clusters. There are even bigger galactic groupings out there than clusters, though. Clusters of clusters called superclusters!

Some superclusters are made up of just a few galaxy groups. Others contain hundreds of groups. The Local Group belongs to a supercluster called the Virgo Supercluster. This supercluster contains at least 100 smaller galaxy clusters, including our Local Group.

Astronomers are finding that even superclusters are just small parts of much bigger galactic structures. A Great Wall is a massive group made up of many superclusters. In 2003, astronomers discovered the largest Great Wall yet. Situated about one billion light years from Earth, the Sloan Great Wall is a vast grouping of superclusters 1.5 billion light years long!

This computer artwork shows how galaxies are connected in clusters and superclusters with voids between them.

Galaxies

Voids

That's Out of This World!

It may sound as if space is tightly packed with galaxies, but there are some empty areas, known as voids. The closest void to the Milky Way is the Boötes Void. This region contains a handful of galaxies, but is mostly empty space. It is around 250 million light years across.

SEARCHING FOR GALAXIES

From 2003 to 2004, the **Hubble Space Telescope** was used to examine one tiny area of space that contained no visible stars. What Hubble found was that this seemingly empty area is actually home to 10,000 galaxies.

Hubble focused two cameras on one point in space. The area surveyed was so small that astronomers described it as being like looking at a section of space through a soda straw. Over four months, Hubble took 800 pictures of this region. When combined, these pictures form an image known as the Hubble Ultra Deep Field.

The Ultra Deep Field image showed that in that one "soda-straw-sized" sliver of space, there are 10,000 galaxies. Hubble observed galaxies of different ages, shapes, and sizes. Some are "near" to our part of the universe, and some are very far away.

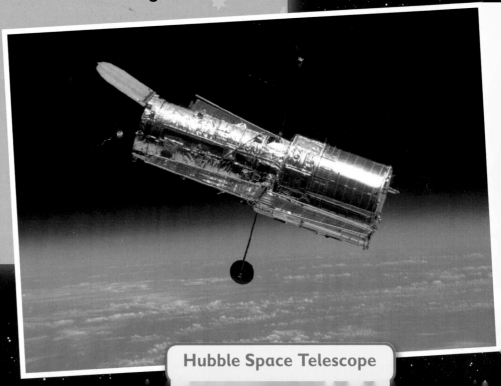

Hubble Space Telescope

The Hubble Ultra Deep Field image shows galaxies of many ages, shapes, sizes, and colors.

That's Out of This World!

So how good is the Hubble Space Telescope's vision?
It's hard to imagine, but if you had Hubble's vision, you could
stand at the US Capitol building and read the date on a
quarter 1 mile (1.6 km) away at the Washington Monument!

LOOKING BACK IN TIME

The Hubble Ultra Deep Field image will help astronomers find out more about galaxies. It will also help us find out more about the formation of our universe because it allows us to look back in time!

Some of the most distant galaxies in the Hubble Ultra Deep Field image are over 12 billion light years away. Traveling at the fastest speed we know of, the light from stars in those galaxies began heading toward us billions of years before the Sun or our Earth came into being. In fact, the light has been heading toward Earth for nearly the entire lifetime of our universe. What we are seeing is how these galaxies looked in the very distant past.

Think of it like this: If we wanted to know what each of those distant galaxies looked like today, we would have to wait 12 billion years for the light to reach us!

That's Out of This World!

Hubble surveyed just a tiny area of space to create the Hubble Ultra Deep Field image. Could Hubble produce an image of the whole known universe? In theory it could. However, the known universe is so vast, it would take one million years!

There are so many beautiful and amazing sights to be seen and examined in our universe. This image shows the Antennae galaxies. They have been colliding for billions of years!

GLOSSARY

astronomers (uh-STRAH-nuh-merz) Scientists who specialize in the study of outer space.

black hole (BLAK HOHL) A region of space around a very small and extremely massive object, usually formed by a collapsed star, within which the gravitational field is so strong that not even light can escape.

dark matter (DARK MA-ter) Material that scientists think makes up a huge amount of the mass of the universe. It cannot be seen, but scientists can detect its presence by the influence its gravity has on other objects in space.

galactic (ga-LAK-tik) Of or having to do with galaxies; of a size and mass that is typical of a galaxy.

galaxy (GA-lik-see) A group of stars, dust, gas, and other objects held together in outer space by gravity.

gravity (GRA-vuh-tee) The force that causes objects to be attracted toward Earth's center or toward other physical bodies in space, such as stars or planets.

Hubble Space Telescope (HUH-bul SPAYS TEL-uh-skohp) A telescope that has been orbiting Earth since 1990. Its pictures of the deepest reaches of the universe are far superior to anything viewed from a telescope on Earth.

light year (LYT YIR) The distance light can travel in a year—more than 5.8 trillion miles (9.4 trillion km).

Milky Way (MIL-kee WAY) The galaxy that includes Earth and the rest of our Sun's solar system. The Milky Way is believed to contain around 400 billion stars.

nebulae (NEH-byuh-lee) *(singular nebula)* Massive clouds of dust and gas in outer space. Many nebulae are formed by the collapse of stars, releasing matter that may, over millions or billions of years, clump together to form new stars.

planets (PLA-nets) Objects in space that are of certain sizes and that orbit, or circle, a star.

solar system (SOH-ler SIS-tem) The Sun and everything that orbits around it, including asteroids, meteoroids, comets, and the planets and their moons.

stars (STARZ) A body in space that produces its own heat and light through the release of nuclear energy created within its core. Earth's Sun is a star.

supernova (soo-per-NOH-vuh) A super-bright explosion of a star that creates a sudden release of energy and light. A supernova can radiate as much energy as a galaxy, and its remains may form nebulae.

universe (YOO-nih-vers) All of the matter and energy that exists as a whole, including gravity and all the planets, stars, galaxies, and contents of intergalactic space. Most scientists believe the universe formed over 13 billion years ago.

WEBSITES

For web resources related to the subject of this book, go to: www.windmillbooks.com/weblinks and select this book's title.

READ MORE

Aguilar, David. *Planets, Stars, and Galaxies: A Visual Encyclopedia of Our Universe.* Des Moines, IA: National Geographic Children's Books, 2007.

Trammel, Howard. *Galaxies.* A True Book. Danbury, CT: Children's Press, 2009.

Vogt, Gregory. *The Milky Way.* Early Bird Astronomy. Minneapolis, MN: Lerner Classroom, 2010.

INDEX